The Truth About Low Back Pain

The Truth About Low Back Pain

THE HIDDEN CULPRITS

Dr Andrew Charles Gorecki

ISBN-13: 9781534809086
ISBN-10: 1534809082

Why Read "The Truth About Lower Back Pain?"

This book was written for you.

The purpose of this book is to help you live a healthier and happier life.

The human body is one of the most complex structures known to man and it can be very difficult to find accurate and helpful information when your body is having a problem. This book is designed to simplify the complex topic of lower back pain.

As a physical therapist AND someone who has personally suffered from back pain for many years, I have a unique perspective that I attempt to share with you in this book. During my experience, I learned that the more knowledge you have about your body and how it works, the easier it will be to live a healthier life.

If you're suffering with back pain and sciatica...and feel like everyone else gets to live life and have fun while you're sitting on the sideline...

Then read "The Truth About Lower Back Pain: The Hidden Culprits"

Use it. Gain Knowledge. Take control.

Yours in Health,

Andrew Gorecki

Physical Therapist

P.S. This book was written specifically for back pain and sciatica sufferers looking to heal naturally without medications, injections and surgery.

If at any time while you are going through this book you don't understand something...or have a question...please don't hesitate to email me directly at andrewg@thesuperiortherapy.com.

Table of Contents

CHAPTER 1

Life as a Lower Back Pain Sufferer

The healthcare system in the United States for lower back pain right now is just simply not good enough.

If you look at the statistics, they are overwhelming...

Right now, we see that over 265 million prescriptions were written for pain medication in 2015. We have 89% of the population in the United States that are going to have back pain at some point in their lifetime. We've got spinal fusions... the surgical rates have increased by 150% in the last 10 years. And only 50% of those spinal fusions are successful two years out... only 50%... imagine that.

My name is Andrew Gorecki. I'm a Physical Therapist and I have been a back pain patient.

In fact, I'm here to tell you a story about my back pain and how I went through the system and my perspective of what the current system is like.

My hope is to also offer some new ideas, new strategies, and new solutions for people that are suffering from lower back pain.

My story begins back in 2006... I was 24 years old. I was a college student. I was very active, very healthy. I lifted heavy weights on a daily basis. I was a runner and a cyclist. I thought I was in the best shape of my life.

Little did I know that one morning I would wake up with extreme shooting pain down my leg. Having no idea what I had done and thinking that it was just going to go away on its own, I ignored it. And I ignored it for several months, but the pain continued to worsen.

I had extreme shooting, burning pain from the back of my hip all the way down to my toes.

In fact, I remember that my big toe was actually so painful that it was throbbing.

Finally, I went into the campus medical center.

I had student insurance at the time and was really struggling financially. I believe it was a 70/30 policy, where I had to pay 30% of the health care cost. I went into the community center and I met with a doctor and told him about my big toe and how painful it was.

He informed me that it was not my big toe, but instead it was my sciatic nerve. I had sciatica...

He prescribed me some Vicodin and some ibuprofen and told me to go home and take them and they would help.

At that point, every daily activity was painful.

I couldn't put my socks on. I couldn't sleep at night. I couldn't sit in a chair or bend over to lift up the toilet seat. Life was a drag.

Of course, the medications helped me, but they only helped for about 5 hours. So what happened was my pain medication became how I told the time of the day. I could tell you exactly what time it was based on how I felt physically.

A month went by and I went back to follow-up with the physician. He asked how it was going and I told him that I was in a lot of pain and things had not changed.

He said, "Let's try another month" and he gave me another prescription for Vicodin and ibuprofen¾and sent me on my way.

As I continued to go about my life, things got worse and I couldn't wait for my next follow-up appointment. I called him two weeks later for an emergency follow up visit.

I told him how much pain I was in. He said that I should go to physical therapy... and as an undergraduate student who was thinking about going into the physical therapy profession, I was very excited.

So I showed up at the physical therapy clinic on my first day...

They explained to me what the sciatic nerve was and why my lower back hurt. And they began to prescribe movements and exercises that made my lower back move more.

As you can imagine, sometimes when you have lower back pain and you move it more, it hurts more...

I was hurting during and after physical therapy, but I was reassured that it was normal and all part of the process and that things would just magically get better.

Over time, I noticed a trend... Sometimes, I would be feeling ok. Maybe the physical therapy would relieve my pain slightly while I was at therapy, but then the pain would return.

This was kind of the pattern that I was seeing. I would feel better for a short period of time, then the pain would come back.

That was very frustrating for me.

About four weeks later, I went back to the primary care physician and told him my story.

He looked at the report from the Physical Therapist and looked at me and said, "You know what? I don't think that you have anything wrong with you. I think that you are just here trying to get pain medication to use it recreationally."

At that point, I sat back and I was completely shocked.

I have never been accused of being a liar before. That was how I felt. I felt I was being accused of being a liar.

So he actually did not give me pain medication and he sent me away.

A couple of things happened that day and the next day...

I began to have increased pain, of course, because I didn't have pain medication...

But I also started to go through withdrawal symptoms. I was sweating. I was very irritable. I couldn't sleep.

The next day, I went back into the office of the physician and I basically just demanded that he reassess me because I was truly in pain.

I was also an exercise physiology major, so I understood the basic principles of the pain response and how that stimulates the sympathetic nervous system.

Things like your eyes will dilate, and your heart rate and your blood pressure will increase, and you will sweat. I pointed those things out to the primary care physician...

He said, "You know what? You are right. You do have symptoms that would make sense that pain would be part of the problem. I'll tell you what...I will give you one more month of the pain medication. But I want you to stop physical therapy and I want you to go to a chiropractor."

I said, "Ok, I will do whatever you say."

A couple of days later, I went to a chiropractor. He examined my lower back and told me that my lower back had segments that were out of alignment and that he needed to readjust my lower back to put it back in alignment.

He said that it was going to take me a long period of time and that I would probably need to see him for three months. He proceeded to manipulate my lower back (which you get the nice snaps, cracks and pops)...

Immediately when that happened, I had an intense shooting pain in my lower back, as well as increased pain down my leg. Additionally, I started to feel numbness in my leg after that visit.

So of course, I went home and I was very upset.

The next day, I called the chiropractor's office and told them about my experience. He told me that was normal and all part of the process...

My gut feeling told me that I should not do that, so I stopped. I waited two more weeks and then went back into the primary care physician's office again, for the fourth time.

He said, "Well, you know what? It is time for you to get an MRI."

I got an MRI. At the time, I think the MRI was $2,000 and I had to pay 30% of that. So I wasn't looking forward to that, but I went in and got the MRI.

Three days later when the MRI came back, it showed that I had a disc herniation at the level L4/L5 in my lower back. I went back to the primary care physician again for him to explain the MRI.

He said, "You have a disc herniation. Here is the problem. The next step is you need to get a cortisone injection at that segment to make the pain go away."

So I scheduled and got the cortisone injection a week later.

Now, it had been about four months of pain, no sleep, no exercise. My quality of life was very poor.

I got the cortisone injection and the radiologist told me that I should feel relief immediately. And sure enough, for about two days, I was completely pain free and very happy. I felt so good that I just started going back to life... I was walking. I was exercising. I was riding my bike to class.

Then on the third day, I woke up and all of the pain had returned.

As you can imagine, I was very frustrated, upset and very discouraged.

I called my physician again (I think it was another week before I could get in to see him). I went in and told him my story... how the injection only lasted three days. And he said, "You really need to try three of them. Research shows that you should try three."

Of course I listened to him. I went back for two more injections over a two week period. Each injection had the same effect - about two days I had no pain and went back to my life with hope... then the pain returned.

Again, very frustrating and discouraging... and expensive.

At my next visit with my primary care physician, he told me that I needed to have a consult with a neurosurgeon. So it took me about four weeks to get in to see the neurosurgeon and it was an experience that I will never forget...

I was sitting in the neurosurgeon's office and he came in... a very busy guy in his white coat and stethoscope. He walked in the door and without introducing himself he said, "Alright, when are we going to do surgery?"

I said, "Whoa, wait a minute. Hold on a second. What are you talking about?"

He goes, "By the time you get to my office, it means that you are ready for surgery."

I said, "Well, I would like to know about the risk factors and the outcomes and what you do during the surgery."

He looked at me and he said, "You know what? I really don't have time to tell you all about that. But when you are ready, you'll know. You just give me a call when you are ready."

He walked out of the office (I think our interaction was less than two minutes).

His nurse came in and I told her how upsetting the conversation was... so she spent a little bit of time explaining the spine anatomy and what a disc herniation meant and what they do during the surgery. So I left the office kind of thinking, "gosh, I'm not really sure what I'm supposed to do. I'm just going to stick it out. I'm just going to live my life and hope this thing goes away."

Another month went by and I was having less and less relief from the medication that was prescribed. So I took it upon myself to start taking twice the Vicodin. Then one night, my wife woke me up (and I was upset because she woke me up)... I asked her, "What's the problem?"

She said, "Well you are not breathing very well."

I said, "What do you mean I'm not breathing?"

She said, "Every minute or so you are gasping for air. You are making me nervous."

I said, "Well, gee that is not good."

She said, "I am going to make you some coffee because I want you to stay up... you are making me nervous. I'm scared for you."

What was happening was I was taking so much Vicodin that I was on the edge of overdosing.

When you take too many opiates, it depresses your breathing and you just basically fall asleep and can die from that.

So the next morning, I called the surgeon and said, "You know what? I'm either going to overdose from pain medication or I have got to have surgery."

He said, "I'll see you on Wednesday."

I went in and had the surgery. It was a very scary experience for me.

I woke up from the surgery and my pain was gone. I was very hopeful that this was the best thing that I had ever done. It was a $100,000 surgery... so I'd pay $30,000 of it plus the MRI, plus the medications, plus the physician visits.

But that was ok. I would do anything to get rid of the pain that I was experiencing and return to my normal life.

The surgeon instructed me that I was not supposed to do anything for the next four weeks. I couldn't lift over a gallon of milk...

So I followed his strict guidelines and I basically locked myself in my apartment. I went from my bedroom to the kitchen to the bathroom on a daily basis. My wife took care of me. I missed classes for a month.

Interestingly, two weeks later, I woke up one morning and all of my pain had returned. I called the surgeon and said, "It is an emergency. I need to see you." He got me in that day.

Again, he spent two minutes with me, but this time, he was a little upset. He started to lecture me about how I must have done something wrong because his surgery was successful and I had not listened to him. I had not followed his guidelines... which I knew was not true - I followed his guidelines very well.

So he was very upset and said, "You know what? I have to do surgery again on you, but I can't even do surgery for another month because you have to heal. The scar has to heal."

I left feeling very discouraged, kind of confused and really upset... afraid I was going to be like that forever. I felt like there was no hope. I was very depressed. At that point, I had gained 35 pounds, I couldn't sleep, and I thought life was over at 24 years old.

It was a very emotional time for me.

It was at the same time that I had just gotten accepted into physical therapy graduate school.

I began school one month later and I was the kid in the back of the class who couldn't sit down, who couldn't really do a whole lot. I had let all of the professors know that my back was an issue.

Students in physical therapy school love other students who have musculoskeletal problems because then they can work on you and learn from you, you are basically the guinea pig... so I had all of the professors and students looking at my body and trying to help me.

Immediately, one of the professors found that my right hip could not rotate inward. It is typically supposed to have 30 degrees of rotation inward. So they began to work on my hip mobility.

About two weeks later, they restored my hip mobility to 30 degrees and guess what happened... my lower back pain and sciatica went away!

Now I didn't know why at the time... and I don't even think they knew why at the time.

But the point of this story is that the entire healthcare system right now is set up to focus on the symptom and the site of the pain.

So in my case, everybody was focused on my lower back as the problem.

I'm here in this book to tell you about new evidence, new science, new treatments that are out there that are proving that the lower back is almost never the problem. It is a result. It is a symptom of an issue elsewhere.

One of Einstein's famous quote states, "Doing the same thing and expecting different results is the definition of insanity."

I would argue that right now, the treatments for lower back pain are insane. The traditional treatments start with medications, then move to injections... then maybe physical therapy. If physical therapy is prescribed, it is usually "traditional" physical therapy that is focused on the site of pain and not looking at the entire body. And then ultimately surgery.

That is the normal sequence right now for lower back pain. We have been doing the same thing for years and years... I would call that insane.

Twenty-five years ago, the standard treatment for lower back pain was putting people in the hospital for two weeks on traction where they would strap the legs and the upper body and pull them apart (which would provide space in the spine).

And that is what we did for years and years and years until evidence came out that showed that that was the incorrect way of going about it. So things evolved and changed.

In 1957, it was proven that abdominal strength - doing crunches or sit-ups - had absolutely no effect on lower back pain. But yet to this day, we still see commercials and products and traditional Physical Therapists teaching people how to strengthen their abdominals to make their lower back pain feel better.

So to me, these things are insane. The system has to change and for whatever reason, it is not changing fast enough. I would argue that there are lots of people that are making money off of the stagnation of the system.

I'm here to share my ideas, my experience and hopefully change the system of lower back pain treatments once and for all.

CHAPTER 2

Top 3 Most Common Types of Lower Back Pain

n this chapter, we are going to dive deep into the three most common types of lower back pain.

Now, we know that there are more than three types, but in fact, 85% of the people that have lower back pain have one of these three types. So it makes sense for us to cover these so that you can get a better understanding of what you may or may not have going on.

The first most common type of low back pain is disc herniations.

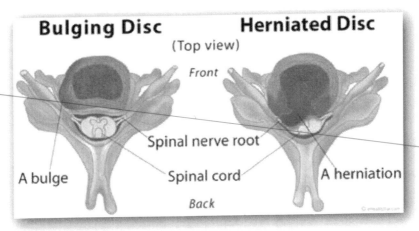

A disc is soft tissue that lies between the bony vertebrae in the spine.

Each level of the spine has a disc and the disc really serves a purpose for shock absorption... and it also provides more mobility in the spine.

A disc herniation is an injury to the disc. A disc has two layers to it...

Imagine it's like a jelly donut. The outer layer is called the annulus fibrosis. It is a very tough outer ring of fibers.

The inner circle of the disc is called the nucleus pulposus. That is more liquid.

The outer material, when you are 25 years old, is more like the consistency of crab meat. As we age, that crab meat material turns to more like leather... so it becomes a little less flexible.

That is going to be important here in a few minutes when we describe the age groups for disc herniations and why it is more common in somebody who is younger.

About 50 years ago, there was a Physical Therapist named McKenzie. He came up with a treatment technique for lower back pain. He believed that the disc could basically be pushed back into place once it had herniated or bulged out.

We used to think that disc herniations were mostly caused by bending forward. So the theory was that as you bend forward, the disc material gets pushed out the back of the spine because there is fluid inside (so the fluid needed somewhere to go). They would call this "fluid mechanics."

There was some cadaver research done in the last ten years that showed that the forces required to tear the outside ring of the disc can be done when we bend forward.

That is definitely possible... but they showed that the outer ring is much easier to tear with rotation.

So when the body or the spine rotates, it takes less force to tear than it does to bend forward.

That is a very important point, because if you remember my story in Chapter 1, the ultimate solution for me was to increase my hip rotation... which ultimately allowed my disc to heal without surgery for the second time.

I didn't have any forward bending injuries. I was simply following my surgeon's guidelines and walking after surgery.

The lack of rotation in my hip actually fed more rotation into my disc, which ultimately led to another disc herniation.

So it is important to recognize that it is easier to tear a disc with rotation than it is with bending forward.

It is also important to recognize that in order to have a disc herniation, that outer ring first must tear. Then the material (the jelly) inside herniates out.

When that jelly or that disc center herniates out, it will push on the nerve that comes out of the spine.

There are these little nerves called nerve roots. The spinal cord actually turns into a nerve root and then travels down a leg or an arm.

In this case, my disc herniated at level L4/L5 and it was pushing on the nerve that traveled down my leg. That is why I had leg pain and numbness and ultimately weakness down the leg.

So how do we know if somebody has a disc herniation?

MRIs show disc herniations... but the problem is that there was also a study done that looked at thousands of random people off of the streets and it showed that 60% of the people who had an MRI showed a disc bulge or a disc herniation. Only 10% of them had pain or symptoms.

I have seen that many times in the clinic, where somebody comes in with evidence...

I have a guy right now where he has evidence of a disc herniation, but that is absolutely not where his symptoms are coming from.

An MRI is useful, but it should only be used as a pre-surgical tool. We will talk about that more later in the book.

How do I know if somebody has a disc herniation without an MRI?

Well, it is very easy. We know that statistically speaking, disc herniations are 85% more common in somebody who is 35 years or younger because that disc material is more flexible and can be forced outward by pressure (like I talked about with the crab meat analogy).

We know that the symptoms are pain, numbness, tingling, and weakness down an extremity. The symptoms would also increase with coughing, laughing, sneezing or in the morning. And there are reasons for that...

The reason that pain increases with coughing, laughing or sneezing is because that increases the pressure inside the abdomen, which pushes more of that disc material outward onto the nerve.

There is more likely to be pain in the morning because our body overnight regenerates or reproduces what is called cerebrospinal fluid - which is the fluid that surrounds the spine and the brain.

So we have 150 milliliters more cerebrospinal fluid in the morning than we do at night. That means that our spine itself is more pressurized and there is more likely to be pressure on the nerves.

There are also very easy tests we can do with somebody that we suspect of having a disc herniation...

The easiest test is called the Straight Leg Raise Test. This is where the person lays on their back and we lift their leg up in the air while keeping the knee straight. That puts the sciatic nerve on tension, and if that nerve is not gliding properly because the disc is pushing on it, the patient will have severe pain.

So there are some simple ways to tell if someone has a disc herniation or not. To summarize they are:

1) Pain, Numbness, Tingling, or weakness down a leg
2) Increase in symptoms with coughing, laughing or sneezing
3) Under the age of 35
4) Pain is worse in the morning than at night
5) Positive straight leg raise test for nerve tension

I can tell you that most people that come into my clinic, regardless of their age, are convinced that they have a disc herniation. I'm not sure of the reason but I think it is easier for us to immediately point the finger at something being structurally "broken" or abnormal in the spine that is causing our pain. If it's broken then I can have a procedure to get it fixed, simple as that. But the reality is that new evidence is indicating that it is much more complicated than that. If we think in terms of what caused the disc to herniate in the first place then we are on the right track.

And statistically speaking, if you are over the age of 35, a disc herniation causing your pain is less likely, especially if you don't have pain traveling down your legs and it is just your lower back.

We definitely see a lot of disc herniations, but I would say they are over diagnosed.

Can a disc herniation be healed?

Absolutely.

Research shows that within six months... with conservative treatment (which includes physical therapy, injections and medication)... that the disc herniation will be healed.

It also shows that surgeries are only 50% successful.

The key to healing a disc herniation is understanding that the outer ring of the disc was torn initially. So we have to look at the person and the movement that they feel may have caused the tear and identify what part of their body has broken down or does not move properly, causing more stress on their lower back.

We will talk about that more as we move forward into the book.

If we don't identify the reason why someone got the disc herniation in the first place, then they could be just like me and it will come back again. That is called Failed Back Syndrome.

The key is to identify where the problem started in the first place.

The second most common form of lower back pain is called SI pain or sacroiliac pain.

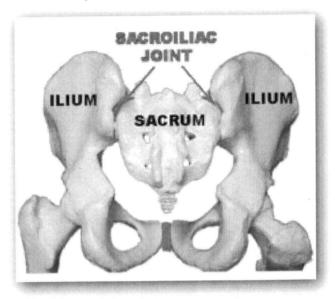

The sacroiliac joint is where the sacrum, which is the bottom of the spine, meets the ilium or the pelvis. It is a joint and you actually have one on each side of your pelvis.

Joints are formed by two bones that come together to form a space and the space is for movement. There is some movement in the SI Joint. (It is not a lot, but there is some.)

When that space and those joints become too small, the movement starts to create friction... and that friction creates inflammation... and the inflammation ultimately creates pressure and then pain.

So this is a very sneaky type of lower back pain because it typically does not show up on an x-ray or an MRI.

It can be very confusing for a lot of medical professionals to diagnosis... but I'm here to help simplify that a little bit.

The most common symptoms of SI Joint pain are:

- It's usually on one side of the lower back.
- It is very localized, so the person can actually put their thumb right on the spot.
- There is little, if any, pain that travels down the leg... but it goes into the groin or pelvic region.
- Pain with sitting is the most common complaint.
- It can occur in all ages of people.
- Very common during, before, or after pregnancy.
- Typically does not show up on an MRI or x-ray.

So how do we manage or how do we deal with SI Joint pain?

We will talk about that moving forward in the book, but ultimately the goal is to reduce the friction in the SI Joint by looking at the areas around it.

Again, the SI Joint is not really the problem... if we are having improper motion in the pelvis or the hips or in the spine, there is going to be friction at this intersection where the SI Joint is formed.

Can SI Joint pain be healed?

Absolutely.

The statistics are actually much higher than disc herniations... we are talking 95% can be healed.

But the approach, again, needs to be looking at the whole body... having a global approach.

The third most common type of lower back pain is called stenosis.

It also has names such as arthritis, degenerative disc disease or disc space narrowing.

Stenosis, by definition, is the Latin term for narrowing.

In the spine, the bony hole where the nerve comes out of, called the neural foraminal hole, begins to narrow as we age. So it actually starts to lose diameter and the space lessens where the nerve itself travels.

Part of this is the natural aging process...

We mentioned earlier that the disc itself starts to get tougher and it actually starts to get dehydrated. When it gets more dehydrated, it actually starts to lose space. It then brings the two bony vertebral columns closer together, and when that happens, it creates the narrowing in the bony hole itself (which can cause stenosis as well).

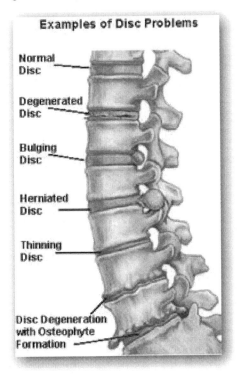

Sometimes people have an accelerated natural aging process in their spine, but I think the most important thing to recognize is that the hole that the nerve comes out of is actually not a fixed hole... it is two half circles that come together to create the circle.

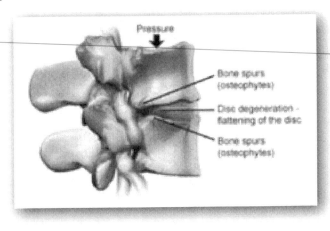

So it is one half circle from the bony vertebra above and one half circle from the bony vertebra below and that creates the circle.

The important part of that is that we know that the hole moves. It is dynamic. It moves when you move.

Very quickly here, we know that there are three ways to make the hole bigger, which would make the nerve happy....

1. You can bend forward. If I bend forward, it makes the hole bigger.
2. You can lean away from the side with the problem. So if it is my right side, if I lean to the left it makes the hole bigger.
3. And if I rotate towards the side with the problem - so again, if I rotate my upper body to the right, that makes the hole bigger.

Now I can make the hole smaller by bending backwards, by leaning towards that side or by rotating away from that side.

It is important to identify that movement is going to influence the diameter of the hole. And the diameter of the hole is going to influence how the nerve feels.

If the hole is smaller, the nerve is going to be irritated. If the hole is bigger, the nerve is going to be happy.

The smaller the hole, the more friction and inflammation there is going to be. The bigger the hole, the less friction and inflammation there is going to be.

Most people who come see me that have a diagnosis of stenosis because of an x-ray, feel like there is nothing that they can do... but that is not the case.

How do we know if somebody has stenosis?

Easy... About fifteen years ago, research was done to create a tool to help us identify if people have stenosis.

So if you have these three things, there is a 97% chance that you have stenosis in your spine:

1. If you are over the age of 55.
2. If you have pain with standing and walking.
3. If the pain goes away with sitting.

That is a very powerful tool... and is more accurate than an MRI.

What can you do about stenosis?

There is nothing that a physical therapist is going to do to change stenosis. Since stenosis is a boney change. We can however understand that the boney changes that occur are in and around a hole that constantly moves and changes its diameter. Therefore, is we can influence how much the hole closes and opens then we can influence how much pain the patient is experience since the hole has a nerve in the middle of it. That is the way to get rid of the dysfunction and improve the motion.

Then, in the meantime, opening up the hole is a way to lessen the symptoms immediately.

Stenosis is very treatable and right now, we are seeing a large number of people that have stenosis and are getting a fusion in their spine.... where the surgeon just basically goes in and opens up the hole and then puts a plate in it to fuse the hole open.

Research is showing that right now, only 50% are successful after two years...

The reason that they are not successful is because if you take away motion at one segment, then the segment above and the segment below have to move more.

More movement starts to create more stress... and more stress equals more stenosis... and the person now needs another fusion at the area above and below.

Fusion is not the answer. I can tell you that.

Instead, the answer is to look at the other areas of the body and try to identify what is actually creating the hole's closure in the first place.

To summarize, the top three most common types of lower back pain are disc herniations, SI pain and stenosis.

All of them are very treatable and there are permanent solutions, but you have to have somebody who understands the conditions and understands that the rest of the body is contributing just as much to those spots and causing those symptoms as the areas themselves.

CHAPTER 3

Top 3 Causes of Lower Back Pain

One of my most favorite topics in this chapter is the top three areas that cause lower back pain.

Before we get into that, let's talk about what the lower back is designed to do. The lower back is the most blamed part of the body and usually the most unfairly accused. With mind boggling statistics like 89% of all human beings will experience lower back pain some time during their life and that the cost of lower back injury is estimated at being over $100 billion dollars each year... it is no wonder why the lumbar spine has been the subject of much accusing and is often referred to as a bad back.

Despite those statistics, I would argue that not only is the lower back not guilty and unfairly accused, but it is often a victim.

The thought process must change on why somebody has lower back pain.

The reality is that the lower back is in a biomechanical chain that is connected to the entire body. It is the crossroads of the body. It lives where everything happens.

It has five individual bones that rest on top of each other with a disc in between.

The typical lumbar spine is designed for only so much motion... specifically, forward bending is 40 degrees, backward bending is 30 degrees, side to side bending is 20 degrees, and only 5 degrees of rotation is available.

What I mean by "available" is that when we get to the maximum limits that the spine is designed to move, the bones actually meet and there is no more motion left.

Some may say that this is a terrible design flaw, but in reality, it is a beautiful design as long as the entire body is moving together as one biomechanical chain.

The lower back has many friends. When I say "friends," what I really mean is it has parts of the body that are around it doing the same thing, at the same time, helping out the lower back.

Unfortunately, sometimes those friends get tied up and aren't able to help...

This happens often times because of a sedentary lifestyle... if we have to sit more than we'd like because of our jobs. This is when the problem starts.

So when the lower back starts to hurt, most people in the healthcare system, as mentioned before, spend all their time and energy looking at the lower back... when in reality, we need to look elsewhere.

We need to find the real reasons why the lower back is hurting.

One quick example, let's say the lower back is hurting, and just below it is under-nourished hips...

If you look at the design of the hips, they have 60-80 degrees of rotation on each side that is available¾a huge amount of rotation compared to the lumbar spine, which we mentioned earlier only has 5 degrees of rotation. So when our body moves, and if our hips are not properly contributing to the motion (especially with rotation), then the lower back is going to be asked to do too much... it is going to step in and help, but it is underequipped.

The lumbar spine only has 5 degrees of motion available. Wear and tear starts to happen very quickly, inflammation starts to rise, and people begin to have pain. But the lower back pain is only a symptom of a bigger problem.

Now on to the #1 area that is affecting your lower back...

Your hips.

The hips, like I just mentioned, are meant to rotate as a ball and socket joint. They have 60-80 degrees of rotation (much more rotation than the segments above). The hips are also designed to move side to side and move more when you bend forward and backward than the lumbar spine.

So the hips are what I would consider the "best friend" or the "BFF" of the lumbar spine.

The problem is, as we start to get older, we sit more. As we are sitting, our hips become tight and rigid and not mobile... so as we lose mobility in the hips, they are not able to help out the lower back as much as they once did. This area then becomes the most limited area for most people and it's because we sit at a desk.

Most commonly, the front of the hips are actually what really make it challenging for the lower back. What we hear from patients, especially as we get over the age of 55 is, "My lower back hurts when I stand or walk. My back pain goes away when I sit down."

That is a big indicator that a muscle in the front of the hips is limited.

It's called the iliopsoas or the hip flexor... that muscle is completely on slack when we are sitting down. Then when we stand up and take a step forward, that muscle has to lengthen. The problem is that the muscle attaches to the hip and the spine. So if it doesn't have the length that it needs to do the activity that you are asking it to do, it is going to pull from the spine. It will then compress the discs and it will cause the spine to extend too much and you will ultimately have pain and compression.

If we want to have a real solution for our lower back, we need to first look at our hips. I hear so many people that have had spine surgeries and injections and medications and nobody has taken the time to look at their hips.

So area #1 that is affecting your lower back is your hip mobility.

The #2 area affecting your lower back is your upper spine.

Looking at the biomechanical design of the spine itself, as you move from the lower spine all the way up to the mid back and neck, what you will find is that the degrees of available motion increase biomechanically. So for every segment that I move up the spine, it was designed for more motion.

That makes sense if you think about it... your neck moves a heck of a lot more than your lower back does.

So if you look at the area above the lower back, it is really common for people to have limited motion in their upper spine.

This can, again, be because of sitting. As we are sitting at a desk and we are fighting gravity, it causes us to have that hunched over posture where you see the rounded upper back (which is called kyphosis).

It is very common for patients who come in with lower back pain to have limited motion in their upper spine.

Again, this area is the #2 "friend" of the lower back.

For example, if I am swinging a golf club and my arms are rotating back, the first things that happen are my arms, my shoulders and then my upper spine have to rotate. Then, as that motion from the top gets driven down through my lower back, it eventually makes it to my hips and my knees and my feet, which are very important in the golf swing.

To break that down for you...

The first part that happens is the motion is driven through the arms and through the mid back.

If that mid back doesn't contribute enough, it is going to ask the next closest place to contribute more... which is the lower back.

Again, the lower back is going to say, "Well, you are golfing and you are rotating. I only have 5 degrees to give you."

So my point is that if we are looking at lower back pain, no matter what type of lower back pain, we have to look at the mid back as a cause.

And if we have not done that and we have not tried to improve the mobility in the mid spine, then we are missing the true cause and we might be setting ourselves up for unwanted and unnecessary injections, medications and surgery.

Moving on to area #3 that is causing your lower back pain, which are your feet.

Now you might think to yourself, "How could my feet possibly be causing my lower back pain?"

The answer is very complicated, but the simplest form of an answer is that my foot motion and stability dictate my hip motion and stability.

So if my body or brain senses that my feet are on an unstable surface, then what will happen is my muscles will inherently create more stability by getting tighter. The tighter that my muscles are in my feet, my legs, and my hips... the less motion that they can have, therefore my spine has to do more motion.

Let's think about this for a second...

If I were to do a forward lunge right now (and you can picture that in your mind), or you can even practice this at home - try a couple of lunges forward....

Now imagine that you do the same lunges that you did on the ground, but you go on ice.

The most common thing that is going to happen is the person lunges slower and not as far. The reason for this is because the brain perceives the surface that you are standing on to be unstable.

The body can sense stability limitations by receptors called proprioceptors.

We know that the ice is unstable, so it is going to create less mobility in our body... therefore, if I have to move, my legs and my feet and hips aren't going to be as mobile because they are trying to be stable. Thus, my lower back is at risk for doing too much motion if I ask it to.

If I have any stability issues in my ankles or my legs I will have less motion in those areas and more motion in the low back.

You could say the same thing with mobility...

When I bend down to tie my shoe laces I have ankle m. motion and lower back motion. If I take away motion at any o. still reach my shoe laces but the areas that could move will move m. to.

Not only are mobility and stability important factors to consider ᴊot and ankle, but also the alignment of the foot and ankle.

We will often see patients that have one foot flatter than the other foot. What that does, is when your foot flattens out or pronates more on one side, that creates a leg length that is actually shorter because the body has to reach farther down to touch the level ground that you are standing on.

This leg length difference often also creates a hip that drops down on that same side.

To recap, you have the flat foot that creates a leg that is shorter... therefore the hip has to drop down towards the ground farther... and then you will hear people say, "my chiropractor or my massage therapist has told me that my hips are out of whack."

Well, the reality is that it's not your hip's fault... your feet are the issue.

So when improving the hip mobility and stability, it is necessary to look at the feet. If you have never looked at your feet and your back is still hurting you, the cool thing is that there is hope...

There is an area that you most likely have not looked at that could be contributing to your problem.

I wanted to mention that if you are interested, we are hosting a free Low Back and Sciatica Workshop. We would love for you to attend the event to learn more about lower back pain and sciatica.

You can learn more and register by going to www.thesuperiortherapy.com/lowbackworkshop.

To summarize, the three most common areas that are causing your lower back pain are:

1. Your Hips
2. Your Upper Spine
3. Your Feet

Remember that the **cause** of your lower back pain is not the same as the **type** of lower back pain.

In previous chapters, we talked about the three most common types of lower back pain, which are stenosis or degenerative disc disease, SI pain and disc bulges and herniations.

Those are different. They do not tell us the cause.

The three areas that cause issues are hips, upper spine and the feet.

Truth: The Cause of Your Lower Back Pain Is Not Found In Your Lower Back, But the Areas Around It

CHAPTER 4

Dissecting The Facts About Lower Back Pain

J ust to share with you some information straight from *The Burden of Musculo-skeletal Diseases in the United States* website (http://www.boneandjointburden. org/):

"Musculoskeletal diseases affect more than one out of every two persons in the United States age 18 and over, and nearly three out of four age 65 and over. Trauma, back pain, and arthritis are the three most common musculo-skeletal conditions reported, and for which health care visits to physicians' offices, emergency departments, and hospitals occur each year. The rate of musculoskeletal diseases far outstrips that of heart diseases and respiratory diseases, which affect about one in three persons, with the majority report-ing relatively easily treatable conditions such as chronic hypertension or hay fever and bronchitis.

The cost of treating major musculoskeletal diseases, which often includes long-term pain and disability, is also greater than for treatment of many oth-er common health conditions. Yet research dollars to identify causes, create new treatments, and reduce pain and disability remain much lower than that of other health conditions.

With the aging of the US population, musculoskeletal diseases are be-coming a greater burden every year. The pages of this site illustrate the mag-nitude of musculoskeletal diseases on the US population, and provide a small slice of the cost and impact on the US economy.

Lumbar/low back pain and cervical/neck pain are among the most com-mon medical conditions requiring medical care and affecting an individual's ability to work and manage the daily activities of life. Back pain is the most common physical condition for which patients visit their doctor. In any given year, between 12% and 14.0% of the United States' adult population (above 18 years of age) will visit their physician with complaints of back pain. Of the 140 million patients with pain last year alone only 40 million had a visit with a physical therapist, who are the musculoskeletal experts in the healthcare system. The number of physician visits has increased steadily over the years. In 2012, more than 52.3 million patients visited a physician with a complaint of back pain, compared to 44.6 million in 2004.

A large annual health care survey is conducted in the United States by the National Center for Health Statistics for the purpose of identifying the incidence and prevalence of select health conditions. Pain from any muscle, joint, or bone (musculoskeletal pain) was reported by 52.1% of persons aged 18 years and older in 2012. Low back pain was the most common, affecting 28.6%; neck pain was the third most common at 15.2%. (Knee pain was second at 18.1%.) The prevalence of back pain has remained stable since 2005, and is measured in response to the question of whether the individual "had low back pain or neck pain during the past three months." Females report musculoskeletal pain more frequently than males (54.6% vs. 49.5%). The prevalence of low back pain and neck pain is highest for person's age 45 to 64 years, while overall, joint paint is highest among person's age 65 years and older, where 7 in 10 report joint pain.

About 1 in 13 persons (7.5%) in the population age 18 or older report they have a physical, mental, or emotional problem or illness that precludes work. Among these persons, 27%, or nearly 4 of the 13, are unable to work due to chronic back or neck problems. Another 1 out of 25 persons is limited in the type and duration of work they can do because of back and neck pain. Three in four persons with pain in multiple areas of the back and neck report work limitations. The estimated annual direct medical cost for all back related conditions was $253 billion in 2012...

Back pain often originates from sources that are not readily identifiable. Many causes of back pain are likely related to degeneration, but the actual underlying cause of a given back pain episode is often uncertain."

Now, the reason that the source of back pain is not being identified properly is because the people they are seeing first, which includes primary care physicians, nurse practitioners, medical assistants, and physician's assistants... they have no formal musculoskeletal training.

They don't have training in graduate school as it relates to the movement system.

Now why in the world wouldn't physical therapists be seeing them when they have pain with motion?

These statistics are absolutely depressing.

It simply proves that the way we have been doing things is not good enough.

We must change the way we do things. We must get movement screens on a consistent basis, we must be treated by musculoskeletal experts faster, and we must see experts who get results and have research to back up their results.

CHAPTER 5

Is There Hope for Back Pain and Sciatica Sufferers? How We Can Tell If It's Possible that a Person Can Heal Naturally.

When you study the dismal outcomes of lower back surgeries (50% failure rate), I can see how it is easy to think there is no hope...

Or even the pain medication epidemic that is currently happening in this country due to painful conditions like lower back pain...

I'm here to assure you that there is hope. That's why in later chapters we put down some success stories in other people's words just to try and share how much hope there really is.

As a physical therapist, one of the first things we look at in helping someone with back pain and sciatica is the activity that produces the pain.

The most common activities that cause lower back pain (in order) are:

- Sitting
- Standing
- Walking
- Going up and down the stairs
- Sleeping
- Getting up in the morning
- Getting dressed
- Leaning forward
- Golfing
- Lifting

- Running
- Crossing one leg over the other
- Putting on shoes and socks
- Stooping or kneeling

So if you have any of these, then we have very, very bad news......There's HOPE for you :)

Truth: If The Pain Is Reproducible, It Is Reducible.

Basically what that means, is if you have pain with motion, then the pain can be relieved by identifying how the motion is occurring improperly and then improving the motion.

Physical Therapists are movement and musculoskeletal experts.

Our entire job is to improve human motion in order to relieve pain. So there is hope for you if you have pain with motion.

If your pain is constant, all the time, and not changed at all with motion... it is more difficult and could be more serious and you would want to get to a physician to be evaluated.

Here's the deal... everyone's body has the ability to heal itself if given the correct environment.

So when someone has pain with motion and it is not healing on its own, the motion is the cause of the pain. We must look at the motion and identify what parts of the body are not moving optimally.

When parts of the body do not move optimally, they place stress on other parts of the body (the lower back).

All lower back pain can heal no matter what type or cause.

The challenge is finding the type and the cause.

This can be done and there is hope.

CHAPTER 6

All Lower Back Pain Has This in Common: Inflammation

nflammation is defined as "a localized protective response elicited by injury or destruction of tissues which serves to destroy, dilute or wall off the injurious agent and the injured tissues. The inflammatory response can be provoked by physical, chemical and biological agents including mechanical trauma as well as psychological trauma."

It is important to understand that inflammation is a symptom of a bigger problem when we have lower back pain.

No matter what the type is, all types of lower back pain have an inflammatory component because inflammation is the first phase of the healing process. Inflammation happens first. But it only happens when the body gets damaged and needs to repair.

The body's immune system recognizes damaged cells and the inflammatory response is there to block off the damage and reabsorb all of the dead cells so that the body can move on and lay down new tissue, new cells and ultimately heal the injured area.

Physical Stress is the first and most common cause of inflammation.

So all lower back pain has a component of physical stress where friction and excessive motion is creating damage to the tissues (whether it is bones, muscles, ligaments or tendons).

We are getting physical trauma that is damaging the tissues and the body responds by getting inflamed.

Inflammation is ultimately then creating fluid pressure around nerves and creating pain signals to the brain. We know that inflammation is normal, but we often times see patients that are in a chronic inflammatory state where the inflammation is not going away...

The reason it is not going away is because the root of the problem is not being addressed.

The second cause of inflammation is emotional stress.

We know that a hormonal response happens when we have psychological stress. That hormonal response releases a chemical called cortisol, which is a stress hormone.

Cortisol ultimately increases the inflammation in the body so that we have more of it. Our body is more heightened... we are more sensitive to damage... the body will get inflamed more aggressively. We know that the emotional state of the individual has huge effects on inflammation of the body.

The third cause of inflammation is lack of sleep.

We also know that lack of sleep has a very large impact on the cortisol levels. So therefore sleep patterns affect how the body responds to damage and ultimately how much inflammation that there is.

The fourth cause of inflammation is poor nutrition.

We also know that nutrition is a very important aspect of what is happening. This is probably the newest topic that is out there.

We know that the foods that we eat can either decrease or increase the inflammation in our body. Foods that increase the inflammation are flours and sugars. So simple carbohydrates, they break down to sugar right in your mouth with the help of digestive enzymes... and ultimately these simple sugars, simple carbohydrates are a going to feed the inflammation response in the body.

As the body tries to break down the agents, the immune cells secrete inflammatory messengers called cytokines.

Depending on where the inflammation occurs and your genetic predisposition, this could eventually result in arthritis, cataracts, heart disease, poor memory, wrinkled skin and ultimately just increased inflammation in the body.

So we want to avoid the simple carbohydrates.

We also want to avoid any foods that we have sensitivities to or are allergic to. That is also going to create this stress response and the hormones for cortisol to increase inflammation.

We know that eating a very colorful diet—reds, oranges, purples, dark greens—these have antioxidants which dampen the inflammatory effect. They help our body build cells.

We also know that eating lean protein is very effective in reducing inflammation. And the opposite would be true... consuming lots of red meat with lots of fat is going to increase our level of inflammation in the body.

Also, beyond the concern of sodium nitrates, red meat contains high amounts of arachidonic acids that can promote inflammation.

Other food sources to consider include eggs and dairy products as well.

Finally, for nutrition, looking at the type of oil that you are using when you are cooking...

We know that we want to avoid refined trans fat, Omega 6 in cooking oil and use more olive oil. Omega 6 oils would include soy, corn and cottonseed oil. Olive oil is a great source of oleic acid making it a powerful anti-inflammatory.

Spanish researchers reported in the *Journal of American College of Nutrition* that people who consume more oleic acid have better insulin function and lower blood sugar. We also know that pasture-fed livestock, flax, chia and hemp seeds, wild salmon (not farmed) or smaller cold water fish such as herring, sardines and mackerels are your best choices of high powered anti-inflammatory foods.

So diet has a huge effect.

A quick review here:

We know that physical stress, emotional stress, lack of sleep and poor nutrition are going to affect the inflammatory response. It is important to identify that because the normal treatments that are out there right now are basically altering the inflammatory response (by things such as cortisone injections, oral steroids, anti-inflammatory medications such as ibuprofen or any NSAIDs).

These are things that alter the body's inflammation response, but ultimately do not get to the root of the problem.

They do not fix the inflammation response because inflammation is a normal phase of healing... so our body is still getting damaged. We are just hiding it. We are masking the problem.

That is really where getting to these four main factors: physical stress, emotional stress, lack of sleep and poor nutrition are going to be ways that people can find permanent solutions to their back pain.

Regardless of the type of back pain, it is important to understand that inflammation is the source of what you are feeling.

So whether it is SI Joint pain, disc herniation or stenosis, all of those have inflammation around the nerve root that is coming out of the spine. If we don't just want to alter the problem, if we want to find a permanent solution, if we want to fix the problem... we need to address the four main factors that cause inflammation in the body.

If we can address that, the body will stop being damaged, the inflammation will stop happening, and we will feel better and will have pain free motion.

If you would like more resources about the four factors that either increase or reduce inflammation, please visit www.thesuperiortherapy.com/inflammation for a free PDF download with the four areas that cause inflammation and then strategies and suggestions on how to help reduce the inflammation.

Truth: Inflammation is a Normal First Phase of Healing. That Means Damage is Occurring That Triggers the Response.

CHAPTER 7

Core Strength Is Not the Answer

f I asked you what is the number one exercise to perform for your lower back, what would you say?

Quick I will give you 5 more seconds......

Ok let me guess.

You immediately thought of a "core exercise" - probably a crunch or sit up... am I right?

Well, did you know that core strength's effect on lower back pain has been disproven?

Not only has it been disproven, but it was disproven in 1957!

So why do so many of us (not just you and me and your neighbor, but doctors, other physical therapists, chiropractors) believe that this should be our first course of action?

I know the answer and it will shock you...

Have you ever seen all the fun gadgets on QVC claiming to give you six pack abs or fix your lower back pain (ab roller comes to mind)?

Of course you have and the answer to why we all believe sit ups fix back pain is because the media has brainwashed us.

Before reviewing the studies (which I hope you do), it is first interesting to note that most of life requires only minimal activation of the core muscles.

During walking, the abdominals have an average activity of two percent of maximum contraction. During standing, trunk flexors and extensors are estimated to fire at less than one percent. Add more than fifty pounds to the torso and they fire at three percent. During bending and lifting muscular activation is similarly low. Given that daily life seems to require so little core strength, perhaps it is not surprising that research interventions to increase core strength have little effect on pain.

The point I'm trying to make is that if you have back pain, you must look at the entire body. You must look at the areas above and below the spine.

Stop listening to infomercials and get help from experts who know what they are talking about.

I would highly encourage you to come to our Lower Back Pain and Sciatica Workshop where we will show you actual research-based ways to improve your lower back pain.

You can learn more and register by going to www.thesuperiortherapy.com/lowbackworkshop.

CHAPTER 8

"Random Exercise Produces Random Results..."

This is one of my favorite quotes from the guru of movement, Dr. Gary Gray. This is a fact that cannot be denied. Research has proven over and over again that physical training—whether it be endurance, flexibility, strength, power—is only effective in the way that you are training.

Another way to say it is that exercise is sport or activity specific.

Let me share with you a story.

Like him or not, Lance Armstrong was one of the best (if not THE best) road cyclist of all time.

He scored off the charts with many tests of endurance that had never been seen before. To this date, he has recorded the highest lactic acid threshold known to man (which is a blood test that measures the level of intensity his muscles can achieve before fatigue).

When Lance Armstrong retired from cycling, he took up running. In fact, the month after he retired he signed up for a marathon.

Without much training for the marathon, he figured he would do just fine because his endurance was so high and he had so much success in the past with cycling.

Well... here's what he said at the finish... "I can tell you, 20 years of pro sports, endurance sports, from triathlons to cycling, all of the Tours — even the worst days on the Tours — nothing was as hard as that, and nothing left me feeling the way I feel now, in terms of just sheer fatigue and soreness,"

Imagine that, one of the best endurance athletes of all time had such a hard time in a marathon that included just regular people like you and me who were by no means top notch, world class athletes.

Now ask yourself - why is that?

Well, science says that training the body only translates to the activity that you are training it for. So his cycling experience and training had no impact on his ability to run long distances. That makes total sense when you listen to science...

Now let's apply that principle to how we rehabilitate and train people who have or have had lower back pain.

The most traditional training is for the "core" - which usually means the stomach muscles.

But remember in the last chapter, I talked to you about how in 1957 it was disproven that abdominal strength had anything to do with lower back pain...

Let's talk about traditional core training as if it might actually help our lower back pain. The most common core exercises have us laying on our backs and flexing our trunk or flexing our legs in order to activate our stomach muscles. Some common names are crunches, sit ups, leg lifts, dead bugs, etc.

The problem with this approach is that you are training your stomach muscles to flex. Now let's do an experiment together...

Stand up and flex your stomach (this looks like you are bending forward), now put your hands on your stomach. Does it feel flabby and loose, or firm and tight? For most people it will be flabby and loose, not because you are out of shape, but because your muscle is doing nothing when you stand and flex forward.

Flexing or bending forward is a motion that is given for free. What I mean by free is that gravity is what is bending you forward and the muscles on the back side of your body are actually decelerating you.

The stomach muscles did not make you flex or bend forward. So why in the world would we train them to do so while lying on our backs?

In fact, if you are going to do that, then there will be no translation to stronger stomach muscles when you are standing because they NEVER bend you forward. The only time the stomach muscles bend you forward are when you are trying to get out of bed in the morning.

So keep doing crunches, but they will only help you get out of bed easier.

What we really need to think about is how we train our core muscles to help our spine function better.

The answer really depends. It depends on the activities that you are participating in.

For the sake of simplicity, let's take walking as an example that we want to train someone to get better at, which would include having no pain during walking.

Walking, by the way, is the most common reason or activity that causes people to have back pain. I would say that our abdominals usually have little to do with the cause of back pain during walking, but sometimes they can be related.

So let's just assume that we have a person who has lower back pain with walking and it's because their abdominals need to be strengthened.

What do the abdominals do during the walking motion?

Well, they control the pelvis and the spine during side to side motion, rotation right and left, and extension of the spine.

So that means that if we want to train our abdominals to be stronger during walking, we need to create those motions and stress the muscles during those activities so they build themselves stronger and learn how to react to those motions.

It is also important to recognize that our exercises must be in a position that looks and feels like walking. That would then mean that we need to be standing and not sitting or lying on our backs.

We also dissect walking and realize that 70% of the walking cycle includes a single leg stance. So it makes sense for us to have some single leg exercises.

And finally, notice that when walking we are moving, so therefore our exercise probably should include some motion instead of holding positions for long periods of time (ex. planks).

All of these strategies then will translate into a core that is stronger and able to help control the spine during walking.

You see how easy that was?

Now if you're a runner or gardener or desk sitter who has lower back pain during those activities, the training for your core would be different. It would look and feel like the activities you are having a hard time with.

That is what I mean by not being random.

You must be specific to the goals that you have when you are exercising. If the exercise doesn't look like anything you ever do in your life, then you should probably stop doing it because it is a waste of time. Unless maybe you are only concerned about building muscle for aesthetic reasons, which in that case, it doesn't really matter what kind of exercise you are doing. Most people, however, are exercising in order to be healthier and to have pain free motion.

If you are interested in finding better ways to strengthen your core that might look and feel like activities you actually want to get better at, I would encourage you to visit our website where you will find many videos that instruct you on ways to strengthen your core. Clicking here would be a good start: www.thesuperiortherapy.com/videolearning

If you are interested in learning specific strategies to eliminate your lower back pain, I can tell you it is most likely not your core or stomach that needs attention... Remember earlier we talked about the hips, the feet, and the upper spine.

I would encourage you to learn more by attending our Lower Back Pain and Sciatica Workshop by visiting www.thesuperiortherapy.com/lowbackworkshop

CHAPTER 9

Is Your MRI Lying to You?

I want to make it known that in order to fix lower back pain and find a real permanent solution, an MRI or an x-ray is not necessary.

In fact, I would argue that it actually makes the outcomes for the patient worse.

I see people on a daily basis who want and feel that they need an x-ray or an MRI so that the healthcare providers that they are working with know exactly what is going on.

The problem with that thought process is that regardless of if you have stenosis, a disc bulge, SI pain (which typically doesn't show up on an MRI or an x-ray)... the idea that an MRI or an x-ray is going to help the provider fix your lower back pain is false.

The reason for that is because all three of those lower back conditions ultimately are a result of a bigger problem.

The bigger problem is what is actually causing damage to the lower back.

I like to use the analogy of an iceberg...

What you see above the water is only 10% and below the water is the other 90%.

As we talk more about lower back pain, what we start to realize is it is not the lower back's fault that it has a disc herniation or SI inflammation or stenosis...

It is the areas around the lower back that ultimately aren't moving properly that are causing stress.

All of the conditions of lower back pain are ultimately a stress response. It is damaged tissue. It is stress-caused damage.

So yes, an MRI or an x-ray helps identify which type of lower back pain you might have, but it doesn't help you find the treatment or the solution for your lower back pain.

In my opinion, and what I tell many patients that I see, is that an x-ray or an MRI should be used as a pre-surgical tool. If all else fails, a surgeon needs to have an MRI or an x-ray to determine what part of the spine he/she is going to surgically alter.

As you noticed, I didn't use the word fix because I think the word fix is a relative term. Any and all lower back surgeries don't fix the problem. They just alter the problem.

Let me share a story of a patient I recently had the opportunity to work with...

He was a local physician who had developed severe sciatica and lower back pain on the right side of his body. He was hardly able to walk. He happened to see our advertisement in the local paper for a Lower Back Pain and Sciatica Workshop.

After the workshop, he came up to me and told his story...

He had recently gone to his primary care physician who offered him pain medications for his symptoms, but he was struggling because legally he can't take pain medications during his work hours. He had also just had gotten an MRI, which showed he had a disc bulge on the left side of his spine. He then had a consult with a neurosurgeon who recommend he have surgery immediately. In fact, he was actually scheduled for surgery the following week.

His question was... How could a disc bulge on the left side of his spine cause pain down his right leg and in his right lower back?

The answer I had for him was... it CAN'T.

He was almost relieved with that answer. Being a physician, he was almost embarrassed that he didn't know the answer or believe the neurosurgeon, but deep down inside, he knew that it was not possible and that it didn't feel right to have surgery.

So he committed to 15 visits of physical therapy and every visit he began standing up straighter, walking without pain and finally was (and still is) pain free.

His big limitation was actually his hip mobility, which was causing increased stress in his lower back. His disc bulge had nothing to do with his problem.

If you remember back to chapter 2... looking at the statistics and the research behind MRIs specifically for disc herniations, what they show is that 60% of people that are given an MRI for any reason will have a disc bulge or disc herniation. But only 10% or those people have pain.

Basically what that means is that the MRI often times can actually confuse the provider and make somebody think that they have a disc herniation or a disc bulge, when ultimately the pain is not coming from that abnormality.

We also know that there is a huge cost with MRIs. The average MRI is over $2,000 and they are only typically valid for less than a year.

They really just don't help as much as we think they help. I would even argue that there are health providers (such as Physical Therapists, Orthopedic Surgeons and Physiatrists) that know what are called orthopedic special tests... which are movements or positions that you put a person in which helps identify what the condition actually is. And research has shown a high level of reliability that these tests can indicate what the source of the lower back pain is or the type of lower back pain that somebody has.

For instance, if I have somebody who I believe has stenosis in the lower back I can give them a verbal questionnaire which has been proven to be 97% accurate.

The questionnaire asks:

#1. Are you over the age of 55?
#2. Do you have lower back pain with standing and walking?
#3. Does your lower back pain go away with sitting?

If you answer yes to all three of these questions, then there is a 97% chance that you have lumbar stenosis.

That has been proven by research and is actually more accurate than an MRI or an x-ray.

We also know that testing for disc herniations and disc bulges would include a test called a Straight Leg Raise or a Dural Stretch Test which stretches the sciatic nerve.

If that is a positive test, there is a 90% chance that the person has a disc herniation or a disc bulge.

The self-test can be found online at http://thesuperiortherapy.com/category/video-learning/self-tests/

We also know that just asking the patient, "Do you have increased pain down your leg with coughing, laughing or sneezing?" Those are very strong indicators that a person has a disc herniation or a disc bulge and is much more accurate than an MRI.

I often have patients who come in with imaging...

They tell me their symptoms and their symptoms don't fit with the image they have in their hand.

You have to disregard the x-ray and the MRI, which becomes a waste of money and a waste of time.

Being confident that research shows that the image may not be true is very important. Trust me, I have seen this happen hundreds and hundreds of times in the past... but yet every patient that comes in the door feels that they need to have that image.

So I'm here to tell you that the MRI and the x-ray often times are lying to you.

It is not the most accurate way to identify lower back pain and find solutions.

In fact, it doesn't help anybody find a solution. It just helps you categorize an individual and tell them what the structural damage is... But it does not tell somebody what to do about it, what the cause is, or what the treatment should be.

It is ultimately a tool that should be used only when somebody is about to have surgery so that the surgeon knows the exact level to go to when he/she is going to alter the structure of the lower back.

I think that it is important to understand that MRIs and x-rays have a purpose, but it is not the purpose that you probably believe.

I'm here to tell you that you should trust the health provider that you are working with and if they don't feel that you need an MRI or an x-ray, then that should be the advice that you follow.

Otherwise, you could end up spending way more money and way more time than you really should be in the first place. And ultimately it just categorizes you and it does not find a permanent solution.

CHAPTER 10

Can Sleep Effect Your Lower Back?

This morning I woke up and my first thought was how great I slept last night. This is a rare event for me lately with a business to run, patients to treat, a toddler who sometimes sleeps all night and sometimes doesn't, and a wife who is about to have another child any day now.

So needless to say, sleep is a rare event.

Last night's sleep was super important though.

I've recently been training for a half marathon that takes place in a few months and two days ago I had my longest run yet... 9 miles.

So naturally, after that far of a run, my body needed some rest and recovery.

Unfortunately, the night after the run my sleep was interrupted many times... I felt especially sore and fatigued the next day.

But today, after a great night's sleep, I can tell my body had a chance to recovery and I am ready to run again.

And when I woke up this morning, I thought about how important sleep is and how I absolutely have to write this down and share it with you...

We all know that sleep is important, but I don't think all of us know how important it is for the healing process.

When we enter sleep, we go through several phases of sleep cycles.

The one I want to focus on is called REM sleep. This is the deepest sleep cycle and lasts only 90 minutes and we usually only get 3-4 cycles of these each night.

REM stands for Rapid Eye Movement, but for the sake of this conversation, I want to focus on what happens during REM sleep.

There are many things that happen, but most importantly, our body releases Human Growth Hormone (HGH) during these cycles of sleep. HGH is responsible for our cell recovery and growth. In fact, this is the only time the body releases these hormones is when we sleep. This hormone is responsible for rebuilding our broken down body tissues. It is essential to healing.

Those of you that have experienced pain know how sleep can be affected and it usually decreases our sleep in total.

I want to point out how important sleep is to the recovery process. I frequently hear people talking about having recovery days as it relates to physical therapy or exercise, but I don't think people understand really how the body recovers.

Most of our painful experiences with any condition, but especially with lower back pain, is related to inflammation.

Inflammation, as mentioned early, is the body's first step in the healing process. It is the step where the body's immune system begins to section off damaged cells and eat or reprocess the dead cells.

Then as we sleep, HGH stimulates the next phases of healing.

A patient that I worked with a few years ago comes to mind... He was recovering from a shoulder surgery and he was not making much progress.

His tissues were inflamed and painful. His range of motion was poor and he was about four weeks behind where he should have been.

As I got to talking with him, I made a comment about how tired he looked. He mentioned that he hadn't gotten more than two hours of sleep in over two months.

At that moment, I stopped his physical therapy session and discussed the importance of sleep. He agreed that sleep was important, but was lacking the strategies on how to get better sleep. So we came up with this...

He was on a regular dose of NSAID's to reduce his pain level. So he decided to take the PM version of his NSAID's for one weekend to see how it went. He came in Monday morning with a huge smile on his face...

In just three nights, he was able to reduce his pain level by 50% and his range of motion increased to a normal level for that phase after surgery.

Unbelievable results with simply tweaking the sleep cycles.

You see, the body has an amazing ability to heal itself. Nobody can do that for it. But it only heals itself when given the proper environment. That environment must include sleep, nutrition, oxygen, and water.

The physical environment is also an important one, but is not as important as the essentials just mentioned.

So with all of that encouragement to sleep, I want to say I understand how hard it can be...

So here are a few tips for you to try and follow to get better sleep to allow for a quicker and more efficient healing process.

1) Go to bed. It is important to make bed time a habit. Habits are created with consistent practice. Setting a bed time is essential to this process, even if you don't think you will be able to fall asleep. Of course it is recommended to get 8 hours of sleep per night, but set your bed time 30 minutes before that 8-hour mark to allow yourself some time to actually fall asleep. I personally set a bed time of 10pm and wake up at 6am. I usually try to get into bed at 9:30 to give myself some time to actually fall asleep.

2) Stay Hydrated. Research shows that if someone is not hydrated properly, they will not get to sleep as easily and will not stay asleep. This is especially important the older we get, because I often times hear people saying that they are frustrated at how many times a night they have to get up and go to the bathroom, so they simply don't drink water before bed. I would argue that going to the bathroom at night is a totally different issue that can be address by following a voiding schedule (we will not cover that in this chapter), but if this is your problem, I would encourage you to look that up online and educate yourself on ways to improve your voiding schedule.

3) The bedroom is for sleeping and sex only. A neuroanatomy professor in graduate school once told me this, but research does back up the idea that removing distractions from the bedroom does allow for optimal sleep. That includes removing TV's or radios or iPhone from your site while in your bedroom.

4) 2-hour break from screen time. New research shows that having your face in front of a screen two hours before bed has a negative effect on sleep. This is because it has an effect on your brain's circadian rhythm that is usually stimulated by sunlight. So no screens before bed.

5) Find a pain free position. This is particularly important for the lower back pain sufferers who just really have a hard time getting to sleep due to pain. There is no right or wrong position to sleep in for your back. Just find one that feels the best. For me, it was laying on my back with pillows under my knees. For you it will be different.

6) Cool environment. Research also indicates that we sleep better in cool environments. So turn down the heat, reduce a blanket or two, take off some layers of clothing and get some better sleep.

I hope these simple tips can help you sleep better.

Remember, it will help your lower back heal faster. You must consider sleep a top priority.

If you would like to learn more about how the body heals itself and what you can do to optimize it, especially when dealing with lower back pain, we are hosting a free Lower Back Pain and Sciatica Workshop.

You can learn more by going to www.thesuperiortherapy.com/lowbackworkshop

CHAPTER 11

How Traditional Medicine (Including Physical Therapy) Is Wrong

Coming from a physical therapist, this might sounds a bit strange… but I am here to tell you that the traditional approach that is being taught at the graduate school level in physical therapy is not good enough for lower back pain patients.

As I have mentioned many times, I am a physical therapist, but I was also a back pain patient for over a year. I had all of the treatments that are available and I can tell you that traditional physical therapy was very disappointing.

Let me describe for a moment what I mean by "traditional"…

In graduate schools all across the country, the approach is very segmented.

Each week you learn the anatomy and physiology of a specific body part and all of the associated problems that can occur. And then the next week, you move on to the next body part.

So week one might be the foot and then week two might be the knee…

There is never a time where someone explains how the foot affects the knee or how to knee affects the hip or how the hip affects the lower back. (Which seems silly because even as little kids we sing the song about the foot bone being connected to the knee bone…)

And as we have talked about in this book, the lower back is not the source of your pain, but only the site of your pain.

The source is going to be above or below the lower back, most commonly the hips, feet, or upper spine.

So what happens in traditional physical therapy is that understanding how the lower back moves allows a therapist to show you ways to decrease your pain... which is important and it does make you comfortable, but it does not allow you to fix the actual problem and return to the activities you once were able to do.

It only treats the symptoms, not the dysfunction.

It may provide you with some relief, but what it really does is make you rely on the person who is putting you into positions of comfort. It makes you rely on physical therapy or chiropractic or massage. It doesn't provide a permanent solution.

I don't know about you, but I don't want to be dependent on anything to live a pain free life.

So let me tell you a little bit more about my story as a lower back pain patient and what traditional physical therapy was given to me.

I was introduced to the lower back pain guru in town who was certified in a special technique called McKenzie.

McKenzie was a guy who 50 years ago was working with patients in the hospital with lower back pain.

Back then, they used to simply put all lower back pain patients on traction in a bed for two weeks (which did provide pain relief while in traction, but has since been shown to be the worst treatment because it fixes nothing long term).

So McKenzie was telling this patient to lay on his back while he was getting the traction machine ready and when he came back in the room the patient had moved onto his stomach.

It's important to note that the bed was also at an incline...

When McKenzie came back into the room, he was upset at the patient and instructed him to roll back over. When the patient did, his lower back pain was gone. It was a miracle.

So from that day forward, McKenzie had all of his patients try laying on their stomachs with an inclined bed.

Pretty awesome science, isn't it?

And the treatment called McKenzie was born.

Now the treatments have evolved over the years, but still have the basic component of "let's move the lower back in certain directions to make it feel better" thought process.

The problem with this approach is that it completely ignores the idea that areas around the lower back are affecting the lower back.

So I was given this treatment for three months with no results. You can imagine that it was very frustrating.

Ultimately this led me to surgery because the surgeon and doctors working my case made the assumption that physical therapy, chiropractic, injections, and massage had failed and was not going to fix my lower back.

The problem is that it would have been ok to say that the specific type of physical therapy failed, but what other types of physical therapy are out there that might have worked?

The surgery did "fix" the disc herniation, but like I have mentioned before, it was back two weeks after the surgery.

It was not until I found a physical therapist who used Applied Functional Science and understood that my hips affect my lower back was I able to find a permanent solution.

Unfortunately, this thought process is still not being taught in graduate schools. You must go onto specialize in Applied Functional Science to gain this knowledge. (Which all of the therapists here are www.thesuperiortherapy.com)

I personally think it should be required and part of the graduate school curriculum because it is the best treatment available for lower back pain sufferers.

The point that I'm trying to make is that not all physical therapy is the same.

Just like not all doctors are the same, not all mechanics are the same, not all dentists are the same.

It is important when you have a specific condition to see people who are experts. An expert is not only someone who works with many patients that have the specific condition, but experts are also people who get good or great results.

This is an important distinction.

I can call myself an expert, but if I'm not getting results, then I am simply a self-proclaimed expert.

I would also say that an expert in the healthcare field must be using treatments that have been shown to be effective in peer reviewed journals.

So when you are searching for an expert, ask these questions:

1) How many patients a year do you see with my specific problem?
2) Do you have statistics on the results that your patients get from your treatments?
3) Do you have any literature from peer reviewed journals that supports your treatment approach?

You can no longer trust information online or in newspapers or even what your doctor tells you.

Just be your own advocate, ask the correct questions, and find an expert in lower back pain.

In Traverse City, MI, the Superior Physical Therapy Physical Therapists are the experts in lower back pain. We are the only physical therapists trained with a Fellowship in Applied Functional Science. 85% of our Lower Back Pain Patients are pain free at the end of their treatment. If you would like to learn more about Superior Physical Therapy visit www.thesuperiortherapy.com/workshop

CHAPTER 12

So Why Haven't You Had Your Movement System Tested?

Most people in the United States go to the dentist every six months. The appointment usually consists of a teeth cleaning, gum depth measurements, an oral cancer screen and sometimes an x-ray to see if you have any cavities.

Most of the time, the results of the six month check-up are that the dentist encourages you to floss more and brush more and maybe gives you specific recommendations for a trouble area of your teeth that you should focus on.

If all goes well, you leave with no cavities and some guidance on where to focus in the next six months to avoid a cavity. Sometimes, however, the dentist does find a cavity and will then schedule for you to have it removed so that you don't have to have an emergency event... which usually leads to a root canal... which can be very painful and expensive.

We also have check-ups for our prostate, our heart, our eyes, our ears, our skin, and every other major system in our bodies.

There is one exception though and that is our musculoskeletal system, or the movement system... which seems a bit weird because I would rather be able to move around in my day than have pretty teeth.

It also seems weird when you compare the musculoskeletal system to your teeth because usually insurance covers musculoskeletal problems, but not usually teeth problems, or at least not as good of coverage.

It seems to me that if the statistics indicate that the second most common reason why someone uses the healthcare system is because of musculoskeletal pain, that we would have a better system in place for testing that system so that we could identify problems quickly and more efficiently than we are doing now.

The solution to this problem is to have a movement screen that is performed every 3-6 months.

Let me explain what a movement screen is...

So we have talked many times in this book about how the lower back pain is only a symptom of a bigger problem. Most commonly, the problem is that your hips, upper back and/or feet are either not stable enough or don't have enough mobility.

This poor motion above and below the spine causes stress and damage over time ultimately leading to the symptom of lower back pain.

So a movement screen must look at all of those areas and see how they move and how stable they are.

Makes sense, right?

Well, there are a few different movement screens out there, so let me talk about what makes a good movement screen.

First of all, we must identify some truths or principles about the way we move:

1) We move in three planes of motion (front to back, side to side, rotate left and right).
2) We typically move when we are on our feet.
3) If movement is what we are measuring, then movement must happen during the screen.
4) The screen must look at the entire body, not just the symptomatic part of the body.

A movement screen should be performed for anyone who is in pain or not in pain.

Ideally, a movement screen is performed when someone is not in pain so that we can prevent the pain from ever starting... but if you are in pain, a movement screen is still the most important first step in identifying the permanent solution.

This screen allows a physical therapist to assess how the entire body moves in three planes of motion in under 10 minutes.

It identifies where you are successful and where you need help to be more successful. It is the movement screen that all of our therapists at Superior Physical Therapy are certified in.

Other movement screens assess someone in the sitting position, or lying on their backs.

I would argue that these are not as effective because our body moves differently when standing and fighting against gravity. Most of our movement problems occur when we are upright and moving around on our feet.

I realize some patients have lower back pain with sitting and then I would absolutely assess someone's movement in the sitting position... but for the majority of people with lower back pain, standing, walking, bending, and reaching are the most common problems.

The problem with lower back pain treatments right from the start is that the focus is on your lower back. The person examines your lower back either with their hands, asking you to move it, or analyses your x-ray or MRI

So right from the start, the healthcare provider is ignoring the rest of the body.

It is ridiculous that we handle problems this way. It would be like if the dentist just drilled out your cavity and then saying, "have a nice day." He would be irresponsible if he didn't tell you in the future to floss more to prevent this from happening or to recommend that you brush your teeth more.

Imagine if dentists never recommended brushing or flossing... wouldn't that be insane?

Imagine if the only time we went to the dentist was when we had pain and needed the drill...

Prevention is the most effective strategy.

So it is my mission to encourage you if you haven't had one to get a movement screen on a regular basis.

Whether you're in pain or not. Whether you want to or not. Go and get it done. Schedule it right now.

In fact, here is our clinic number so that you can take action - 231.944.6541.

Simply say, "I want a movement screen."

CHAPTER 13

What Can You Do? (Especially When You've "Tried Everything"?)

By far the most common treatments for lower back pain are medications, injections and surgery.

All three of these treatments are 100% focusing on the symptom of pain, inflammation, or structural damage in the spine.

But if you have been paying attention at all during this book, you know that there is a bigger problem going on above and below the lower back that is creating the inflammation or structural damage that is being ignored...

This is the true injustice that is happening out there.

It is the offer of a solution and on the surface, it provides people with immediate feedback of inflammation reduction or pain reduction so that people feel that they solved the problem, but it is false hope.

It has been proven over and over again that the two year successful outcomes of these types of treatment are only 50%.

It's not because they were bad at giving an injection... or the surgeon did a bad surgery... or that the medication was an ineffective drug.

No. It's because these treatments didn't fix the problem, they only altered the problem for a later date.

So should you simply avoid medications, injections, and surgery?

No, they all have a place and can be very helpful at controlling our symptoms... but if these treatments are used alone, then the outcomes will not be as good as if they were used while trying to identify the true cause.

In the case of lower back pain, it is usually a movement problem.

So the most effective strategy that I see is a combination of medication, injection, and physical therapy.

Surgery, in this case, should be used only as a last resort when everything has been tested in combination and tried for a long period of time (to me, that's at least a year).

I see countless patients who try physical therapy for a few weeks and then jump right into surgery.

It is sad when I see that because I know the movement problem has been developing over years and the expectation to eliminate a movement problem in a few weeks is just simply not going to happen.

Even science backs up strength gains, or flexibility gains, or the phases of healing taking a minimum of six weeks and that's just the beginning... three months is a more realistic timeline.

And that, my friend, is the problem...

When we have pain, we are very motivated to eliminate that pain as quickly as we possibly can. People don't want to wait three months for their hip mobility to improve so that their lower back pain goes away.

We are an impatient society and that's why medications, injections and surgery are so popular, even though they have such low success rates....

It is also important to recognize that the motivation we get from pain can be used positively and usually makes us seek out help.

Once that pain is gone, people become less driven to continue to work on the problem that is ultimately creating the symptoms.

That is the #1 problem with treating the symptoms by using medications, injections, or surgery... once people feel "better" (because they have less pain and inflammation), they think they are cured.

They think the problem is gone because the pain is no longer there.

This false sense of hope allows people to return to all of the movements they once could not do secondary to pain.

But the body knows differently... it is still dealing with the stress of bad movement. It is still wearing down at an abnormally fast pace. So what you get is a patient who two years later is worse than ever because they have been altering the problem and not fixing the problem.

So what can you do?

We must think of pain as being very valuable information that our body generates.

Anytime in life when we receive information, we have a choice of what we can do:

1. We can ignore it
2. We can try to change it or alter it.
3. We can handle it

Ignoring the pain is the easiest and most common mistake that people make.

Simply ignoring the problem, hoping that it will go away, often times results in a bigger problem.

Truth: Pain Has Very Valuable Information and Should Be Used as Motivation.

Another common mistake that we were just describing is altering the problem by falling for the trap that the medical system has set up for us... that is altering the pain signals by taking medications, injections, or surgery.

Anti-inflammatories alter the body's response to inflammation, but remember in earlier chapters, we talked about how inflammation is the body's first response to the need to heal.

So something triggered that need...

It doesn't just happen for no reason.

Or maybe you are taking pain medications (like 265 other million people in the country) which simply alter the pain signal being sent to the brain.

Again, this offers no solution. Maybe you feel better with a hot pack, hot shower, or hot tub, but again this alters the symptom. Usually someone trying this strategy does indeed find relief, but only for a short period of time.

If we are looking for a long term, permanent relief and a healthier body, we want to address the cause of the pain. A good doctor of physical therapy can easily identify the cause of the pain. We call this a movement dysfunction diagnosis.

The goal of forming a physical therapy diagnosis is to find a permanent solution. The goal of a medical diagnosis unfortunately is not - the goal there is to categorize the symptom so that others in the health care community can communicate the symptom to each other.

When we meet a patient in physical therapy, they are usually feeling confident in their doctor's medical diagnosis. For this example, let's just say the diagnosis is arthritis. Unfortunately, they may have also fallen into the trap of believing there is nothing that can be done for arthritis.

This is not true. Let me say that again, this is not true.

Often the diagnosis and the potential or ability to heal are not directly related. If 10 people are suffering from arthritis in their lower back, they may have 10 different responses to physical therapy.

When we handle the cause of the pain, you will know it because you get long term permanent relief that frees you from needing the help of doctors or physical therapist or chiropractors or massage therapists.

Truth: The Most Effective Strategy to Eliminate Lower Back Pain Is to Handle the Problem.

Applying this truth...

So this means that you must make the choice to stop ignoring the problem and seek help of a professional (and in this case that means a physical therapist).

Healthy people address pain as soon as possible. Unhealthy people ignore pain or try to alter it. This is no different than any other area of our life. Have you ever ignored a problem and it magically went away? That would be rare.

Relationships, marriages, finances, health or the conditions of our life rarely get better when we ignore it.

So to review, you have three choices:

1. Ignore it. No more explanation needed.
2. Try to change it. You can sit in a hot tub, use a heating pad, take an anti-inflammatory, pain medication or whatever other method you have. Often sometimes it is as simply as "resting" for a few days. Yet the pain will likely come back. Why? Because you have not handled the problem.
3. Handle It. You must ask for help. The human body is so complicated and requires experts in the area that you are having trouble with. ..

You can call your physical therapist that is trained to find the problem and not the symptom.

Questions for you:

1. Can you think of other times in your life when you ignored a problem? What was the outcome?
2. Can you remember a time when ignoring a problem actually made things better?
3. Can you think of a time when you treated the symptom of a problem and that fixed it?

CHAPTER 14

The Single Biggest Mistake Low Back Pain and Sciatica Sufferers Make

10. "My _____ had the same problem." (fill in the blank with mom, dad, sister, brother, uncle or relative... What do they have to do with you? Well, it's genetic right... well everything is 50/50. 50% genetic, 50% your environment and the choices you make.)
9. "I've always had a bad_____."
8. "I have arthritis."
7. "I have fibromyalgia"
6. "I don't have time... I'm too busy."
5. "My body is different than everyone else's... there is something wrong with me."
4. "It's an old injury... nothing can be done about it now."
3. "I have already tried everything."
2. "I do physical therapy already... I got exercises off the internet."
1. "I had an MRI and I have a disc bulge (stenosis, degenerative disc disease, etc.).

Sound like anyone you know?

The reality is that the biggest mistake people make when they have lower back pain is that they make excuses...

It is not normal to live with back pain. You should expect to heal and be pain free. Let me repeat that again.

It is not normal to have lower back pain and you should expect to heal.

Our bodies are designed to heal. You wouldn't expect an open cut to never heal. When given the right environment, everyone's body will heal.

This is the same for every single human on earth, you are no different.

Sometimes we are not even aware of our excuses.

What I mean by that is that sometimes our excuses are non-verbal, but they are expressed through our actions. As a physical therapist, I see it every day...

I call it the "Onion Analogy."

Life is like a four layer onion.

Think of each layer of the onion starting from the outer layer and moving into the core or center.

The outer layer includes the activities that involve movement that we do recreationally: tennis, swimming, softball, running, gardening, playing with our grandchildren, etc. These activities give us pleasure.

The next layer to the onion is activities that we must do every day or activities of daily living. They include working, cleaning the house, and yardwork. It's stuff that we might not like, but we must do.

The third layer of the onion as we move in toward the center includes basic activities such as standing, walking, laying, sitting.

The core of the onion includes essential activities such as sleeping, eating, drinking.

As we start to have pain, it usually first becomes noticeable and effects the outer layer of the onion... those activities that are fun, but not essential and we can live without.

We begin to slowly reduce how much of those activities that we do - I call it activity avoidance. Sure, your back is good all day except when you play tennis, so now you have eliminated tennis from your life or play it less frequently.

As we continue to ignore the problem, the list of activities that we are avoiding starts to grow.

...slowly entering the other layers of the onion... until we get to the deep layers that begin to affect our everyday essential activities, such as sleep or laying down or sitting.

That is the most common time we see people begin to ask for help with their lower back pain.

So the list of activities they have been avoiding is huge and now they are so painful that it doesn't matter what activity they do, they are in severe pain.

This, my friend, is not the best strategy, but it is the most common one.

The problem is that now it is going to take much longer to create an environment for the body to heal and the person is suffering.

When someone is suffering, they are much more likely to fall for the trap of medications, injections, and surgeries.

Healthy people get help when problems first begin; unhealthy people ignore problems or make excuses.

Truth: The Biggest Mistake People Make is Making Excuses.

CHAPTER 15

What Successful Treatment for Lower Back Pain Looks Like

You can walk into any pharmacy or supermarket and find a million different treatments for pain and lower back pain specifically...

The latest gadgets and gizmos for back pain on TV daily...

Famous people endorsing all sorts of wacky treatments for lower back pain...

The options are overwhelming, especially if you are not aware of how to sort through the mess.

Here's a small list of what is available for lower back pain:

- Heat
- Ice
- Medicine (anti-inflammatories, muscle relaxers, pain killers)
- Surgery
- Injections
- Herbal remedies
- Joint juice
- Vitamins and supplements (ex. glucosamine)
- Massage
- Physical therapy
- Chiropractic
- Electrical stimulation
- Ultrasound

- Lasers
- Creams/ointments

From what you have read so far, you know that none of these options provide permanent relief because they only treat the symptoms of pain or inflammation.

So the real answer is to do research on the most successful treatment available.

Research through the use of scientific articles that have been proven using the scientific method and then reviewed to make sure they are accurate and valid have been proven to find successful treatments.

Research that has proven what has worked on other people.

Physical Therapists only use treatments that are proven by research.

All of the other options listed above do not have to follow that guideline.

So I went ahead and compiled what research says to be true.

Before we get into the details of that research, let's step back in time for a minute.

Remember back in the 1950's and 60's... What was the standard treatment for lower back pain?

BED REST.

(Days upon days, which turned into weeks of bed rest.)

Well, luckily, we now know that research proves that bed rest is actually likely to cause more harm than good.

The latest research shows that one of the best things we can do for back pain is keep moving!

Why does exercise improve back pain?

There are many reasons, but the two main reasons are (1) that moving increases blood flow, which is necessary for healing and (2) moving in the right way will actually fix the movement dysfunction in the areas above and below the spine, reducing the stress in the lower back and allowing for healing.

So physical therapy provides us with prescriptive movement that can help us heal lower back pain.

What does successful physical therapy treatment for lower back pain look like?

We know not all physical therapy is the same, so we must identify what is the best type of physical therapy for lower back pain.

I know that we have spent a lot of time so far in this book talking about what things are NOT ideal... and the way things can improve... and giving information about lower back pain… and the current treatments that are out there… and how most of the time they are really just altering the problem…

Understand that we really have three ways to address a problem:

1. We can ignore the problem.
2. We can alter the problem.
3. We can fix the problem.

The reality is most of the treatments that are out there right now for lower back pain are simply altering the problem.

The list of altering goes on and on and on. It includes medications, injections and devices such as traction or inversion tables. All of these things are designed to alter the symptoms of lower back pain.

So what does successful treatment look like?

I think it's important to identify a couple of principles of what successful treatment looks like.

The first thing that successful treatment needs to include, or the first principle, is understanding that we need to identify the dysfunction first, instead of simply the symptom.

Earlier I talked about the top three types of lower back pain: SI pain, stenosis and disc herniations or bulges.

Those are really just identifying the symptom… but it's important to identify the dysfunction.

We know that there are three main areas that are often times dysfunctional when someone has lower back pain.

We know that the areas above and below, if not moving properly, are going to cause stress on the lower back.

And if we have stress on our lower back, then our lower back is going to break down and the tissues are going to become damaged and inflamed. Then we will have a symptom.

So the first principle, again, is identifying the true cause of the dysfunction.

This requires looking at the entire body… most commonly the upper back, the hips, and the feet and ankle complex are the areas that are dysfunctional in people that have lower back pain.

That is the first principle.

The second principle that we must identify is what I would call individualized treatment.

Individualized treatment means that each person that comes in the door has something unique about their mind, body and spirit... specifically what are the movements or positions that cause the pain that someone is having.

For instance, if I have a 75-year-old gardener that walks in the door and she complains that when she is bent over gardening, her back is hurting... versus a 65-year-old person who has pain in the lower back with walking.

Those are two different activities.

Walking upright has completely different motions that are happening in the hips, the foot and ankle complex, and the upper spine.

There is a more upright posture. The front of the hips are being lengthened. The ankle complex is being flexed, relying more on the flexibility of the posterior structures. Then of course, the upper spine has lots of dynamic motion when we are walking, but mainly rotation.

If you compare that to the gardener, the gardener has a very bent over posture. Typically on their hands and knees or standing and flexed forward, the hips now have much more flexion in the posterior structures of the hip, and are required to be lengthened versus the anterior.

The treatment must be individualized to the person as an individual, as well as the activities and positions that they are having a hard time with.

So the second principle is individualized and it is very, very important.

We must first understand what the person is having a hard time with versus trying to make them fit into our arbitrary testing and our screening and telling them what "normal" things are.

The reality is, what they are having a hard time with is the most important thing to them.

They don't care about what we believe to be normal. They want solutions to their problem, so being individualized is an important concept.

The third principle of what successful treatment looks like for lower back pain is one-on-one treatment.

This is really going to be targeted at traditional Physical Therapists.

What we are seeing in the healthcare environment right now is a system that is rewarding or paying for volume.

In physical therapy, we have time-based codes. For every 8 or 15 minutes that you are in physical therapy, depending on the insurance company, PTs are paid for that.

We also have rules and regulations that dictate that we have the ability to see four patients at the same time.

When you have a scenario that a physical therapy clinic (you'll see this in physician offices as well) takes advantage of that, now you are dealing with four patients at the same time and typically the provider would hire support staff (which would be called technicians or assistants) that have a lower level of education or understanding. They will be there to assist the patient, but the patient ultimately is not seeing the provider or maybe for a very small limited time when they come into the clinic.

So the treatment is not one-on-one. You are not getting the expert. You are getting the assistant.

So one-on-one becomes a very powerful strategy and it is not just because of the higher education or knowledge a provider may have…

It's also the continuity of care.

When I see a patient in the clinic, as a Physical Therapist, I know that I am more effective when I can see that same patient two or three times a week for an extended period of time. I get to focus on them. I get to remember everything about them. I get to know them better than they know themselves.

One-on-one treatment is really, really powerful. The problem is that most patients don't understand that they have the choice to go to places where it is one-on-one or not.

You should ask yourself as a consumer, am I getting one-on-one treatment in all things healthcare.

Am I getting it when I go to the doctor's office?

Am I getting it when I go in and get an x-ray?

Am I getting it when I go to a Physical Therapist, or a chiropractor or whatever I am doing?

One-on-one is my recommendation.

We are all going to have to fight that more and more as our healthcare system changes and reforms and continues to modify itself…

Because right now it rewards people for not being one-on-one, but for utilizing support staff.

To me this is just not the best way to treat lower back pain.

The third principle that I believe is important in successful treatment is what I would call educational or empowering.

The point here is that in order to make a change, we know that the change really is a habit.

If you look at all of the studies out there, it takes about 60 days to make a habit. I very rarely get to see somebody for 60 days as a Physical Therapist, so I need to teach you what to do specifically so that you can make a change and you can create a habit.

That habit is not only going to help you eliminate or fix the problem, but it is also going to help you prevent the problem from coming back in the first place... because the reality is, something in your environment created the problem in the first place.

Most commonly it is because we have people who sit at a desk too much. Then I teach them ways to counteract the sitting position by moving and stretching the front of the hips out periodically throughout the day limiting lower back pain.

Ultimately we need to educate people on what to do. So every time I have a patient in here, every visit that I have, we have education that empowers a person to be able to make a change.

I believe that the fourth most important principle is that we must educate.

What you will notice, again, is that as the time becomes shorter and shorter with a provider, there becomes less educational time.

I don't know if you remember my story back in the beginning of this book... how I talked about the neurosurgeon that came in and when he walked in the office, he offered me surgery right away. I was very nervous and very scared and I wanted to be educated. He basically said that he didn't have time to educate me.

I actually believe that to be true.

The way that his schedule was set up for that day, he probably didn't have the time to talk to me and educate me.

I believe that successful treatment of lower back pain is educational. I would say that is important.

So educating using models and anatomical figures and diagrams and having conversations...

The world that we live in right now, I would call it the information age. The problem with the information age is that there is so much information out there that it becomes hard to filter through what is actually going to have a positive impact or not.

The best way to decipher the information is to ask the experts who have been trained in what is called evidence-based practice.

Evidence-based practice means that we educate people on what many research studies show to be true. So what science proves is what we educate.

I also want to say that if you are interested in education for lower back pain, we do have a resourceful website. If you go online to www.thesuperiortherapy.com/

videolearning, we have over 250 educational videos about all kinds of diagnoses, but many specifically for lower back pain. So please visit that site if you are interested.

Moving on to the fifth and final principle of what I believe successful treatment for lower back pain looks like...

We really have two main treatments in physical therapy:

We have the hands-on Physical Therapists who do a lot of soft tissue mobilization and spinal mobilizations and manipulations (this kind of falls into the chiropractic category as well).

Then, of course, you have the Physical Therapists that are moving and exercising you.

Research shows that a combination of hands-on physical therapy with functional movement is the most successful.

There was a study that came out in 1999 looking at spinal manipulation... the hands-on aspect of lower back pain treatment.

It showed that for acute lower back pain (less than 16 days old) without pain traveling down the leg, spinal hands-on manipulation was very effective 85% of the time. Anything after that 16 day mark is not very successful, so that is where the evidence and research shows that prescriptive movement that is identified at treating the dysfunction is much more effective than hands-on therapy.

I use an analogy for most of my patients here that makes a lot of sense, I believe.

The body is 88% water. We know if the rain falls on a hill, the water is going to find the valley. The reason that the water travels down the valley is because it is the path of least resistance. When we move, our bodies are the same way.

Our bodies will always take the path of least resistance.

When you look at somebody who has tightness in their hips or tightness in their upper back or both, the path of least resistance becomes the lower back.

So when you are giving somebody prescriptive movements in order to increase the mobility of their hips, the body (if just told what to do) is going to take the path of least resistance... which is through the lower back and it is going to cause the person to have pain.

That is where the hands of a Physical Therapist come into play...

We must use our hands to facilitate motion in the right place so that it doesn't take the path of least resistance through the back.

So we must protect the lower back while the person is moving their hips in this example.

The fifth principle is a combination of hands-on and functional movement. It is very, very effective at helping somebody make a change in their body so that their lower back pain is not painful.

Reviewing the five principles of successful treatment:

1. Identifying the true cause of the dysfunction by looking at the entire body
2. Individualized treatment
3. One-on-one treatment
4. Educational treatment
5. A combination of hands-on and functional movement treatment

One more thing that I want to add... if you are not getting these five things, you can choose to go and get it somewhere else.

You are the consumer.

You always have the power to choose WHO and WHERE you are getting treatment from.

I encourage you to look up somebody else if you are not getting the right treatment.

Truth: Successful Treatment is One-on-One, Individualized, Educational, Whole Body, and Hands On.

CHAPTER 16

Success Stories

This chapter is designed for you to hear others who have come to our Lower Back Pain and Sciatica Workshop and then received treatment from our Low Back and Sciatica Specialists at Superior Physical Therapy. They are real people who have had success. While reading about these success stories try to imagine what your life would be like without pain. Realize that there is hope and there are treatments you have not tried that are successful. If you have any interest in attending the workshop that we host that these people came to simply visit www.thesuperiortherapy.com/workshop for more information.

"I was in a car accident in 2013 and received a whiplash and a fractured sternum, which resulted in chest and back pain, headaches and some breathing issues. I already had some issues with arthritis and of course, this interrupted my life... and my sleep. I came to the October 2015 Low Back Pain Workshop after having been on a short vacation to Myrtle Beach, where it had been painful to sit, walk, lie down, tie my shoes... and I needed help getting in and out of the car. My biggest take-away from the workshop, was there was hope for me. I started coming to PT here in November, and I realized just how limited my mobility and ROM really were. I've always known that the knee bones connect to the hip bone...but I could see, experientially, that "Imbalance influences the whole body." I appreciated the explanation about pain-symptoms-cause-and dysfunction. They don't just treat the symptoms...they see the dysfunction and then go after the cause. I love their hands-on approach at Superior. I love the explanations and instruction they give and simple, do-able home exercises. I love that these Physical Therapists have several ways to get your body to move. So if it's painful one way, they will implement a way for you where there is little or no pain. I have seen improvement in mobility and Range of Motion...I am back to walking a few miles at a time (without paying for it in pain)... I can stand for longer periods of time without pain, I can tie my shoes and find it much easier getting in and out of the car. I know some stretches/exercises to relieve pain if it shows up. And, my sleep has improved. And that's a big deal! Thanks to the great team at Superior PT; I will definitely keep sharing my experience at Superior with my Friends!" - Anne Smith

I started at Superior Physical Therapy 90 days after spinal fusion surgery, L-4 and L-5. I had been in a back brace since the surgery and this was my second back surgery after having surgery 2 years prior.

I didn't know what to expect. Prior I kept active, golfing, running, biking, water skiing, downhill skiing, and cross country skiing. I have been amazed at my progress! I had been through lots of P.T at other places, Superior was completely different. Each visit felt like finding the target to where I was weakest and working at that point. I was given videos and printed directions on how to work at home. This was huge to continue improving and were easy to do at home without any equipment. I feel like I'm back, made of steel, Nick calls me "RHB" or 'rock hard body'. I will continue just once a month maintenance, and I cannot express enough how much this physical therapy has helped me! –John Hanford

"I owe many thanks and praise to Andrew at Superior Physical Therapy for giving me the ability to finish out my half marathon training pain free. Half way through my training program, I started to experience "popping" behind my knee with tightening in my calf which would result in my whole leg going numb. At this point I was not even able to finish a 3 mile run when I was scheduled to be running 6. After another unsuccessful run, I finally had enough and went to see Andrew. Within 10 minutes of doing simple tests and stretches, he knew exactly what was wrong. Within 2 days of performing the exercises he gave me, I felt amazing. Not only was I running pain free but was able to increase my distance and cut down on my time. I will never try to "fight through the pain" ever again! Thanks Andrew"

Sandy came to physical therapy with pain in the left hip and SI Joint which increased with walking and standing for any length of time. In the past, the treatments this patient experienced chased the pain and symptom of SI pain, which gave her relief, but only temporary.

Our treatment approach focused on the dysfunction that was in the hips and thoracic spine, which has proven to give her a permanent solution to her pain...

"I have been in pain for years! I have participated in a lot of physical therapy. However, this is the first time the problem in my hip and foot has been addressed to absolutely AMAZING success! I no longer have pain in my sciatic nerve; I can walk normally for the first time in over 15 years! The therapists here are extremely knowledgeable, caring and are solving a very serious problem I've had for many years. I am so grateful and appreciative! Come here for help!!" –Sandra L. Goetz

Having dealt with back problems for many years, I am no stranger to physical therapy, yet what I encountered at Superior was unique in my experience. Scheduling was easy, and many of the exercises were tailored to my situation rather than simply going through "standard" procedures. Above and beyond just focusing on the problem at hand, what I learned will help me keep my back on the "straight and narrow", so to speak. The entire staff was great to work with, but a special shout out to Ben and Brooke (with a tip of the hat to Adam). You made it fun. If I'm ever referred to physical therapy in the future, I won't even consider going anywhere except Superior. These people are hitting on all cylinders.-Ed Rooney

"Dear Ben and Mike,

I want to thank you both for helping me to get ready for back surgery and then rehab following the operation. You always met me with a smile. PT with you pushed me to my limits but was always mindful of my limitations. "How are you doing, how does that feel, need a break" were a part of every session. That said, it was also good to hear you say, "can you do one more rep?" I never felt coddled or pushed too hard.

Your enthusiasm and humor made each session more fun than work (usually). That carried over to the office staff as well. I was always greeted upon arrival and "have a good day" when I left.

Scheduling called several times to "fit me in" with more convenient appointments.

My list of exercises are doable at home. I understand the importance of doing each one accurately and consistently. It is a priority for me and along with my yoga is becoming a daily routine.

Over the last 10 years or so I have worked with at least 7 different physical therapists around Traverse City. Without reservation you two and Superior PT as a whole have been the best experience. I will not hesitate to recommend you and the office to friends." – Lorraine Brickman

"I am so happy to have my life back! My back was killing me to say the least. When I came to a Saturday back pain clinic I was in pain that no words can describe. I couldn't sit, stand, lay, or find any position that wasn't painful. I came in the following week and started P.T. with Brooke. Come to find out my back pain starts at my foundation, my feet, and then moves up to the back. Brooke gave me some terrific stretches to do at home along with working out my kinks in the office. After a month I am back to my normal self! Thanks a million!" –Lisa Meleski

CHAPTER 17

Top 3 Home Exercises for Stenosis

f you have pain in your lower back or down your leg and the following:

- Pain with standing or walking
- Pain relief with sitting
- Are over the age of 55

There is a 97% chance you have lumbar stenosis. If that is the case here are some exercise ideas that have helped others in the past. They focus mainly on your hip mobility and upper back mobility address the real movement dysfunction that is causing your symptom.

Hip Flexor Stretch: The front of the hip is the most common area in people with stenosis to get restricted or tight because of sitting. This muscle attaches to your spine so that when you stand up it pulls your spine and can create pain. Try this simple stretch but please place a pad or pillow under your knee to prevent knee pain.

How to do it:

1. Half Kneeling on soft surface
2. Gently move hips forward and back, side to side, and rotate right and left - 30 seconds each
3. Repeat on other side
4. 2-3 times per day

Lower Back Stretch: This stretch opens up the hole where the nerves comes out and can provide immediate relief for people with stenosis.

How to do it:

1. Seated at front edge of chair
2. Reach both hands towards ground
3. Hold 20 seconds
4. Repeat 4-5 times

Groin Stretch: The inner thigh is a very common area that gets tight and reduces hip motion which then creates more stress in the lower back.

How to do it:

1. Place one foot on chair pointing forward
2. Other foot is perpendicular on the ground
3. Hold onto structure
4. Move hips gently toward chair until groin stretch felt, 60 second hold

CHAPTER 18

Top 3 Home Exercises for SI Joint Pain

H ip Flexor Stretch: Again the front of the hips can cause limited motion in the hips and more stress on the SI joint.

How to do it:

1. Half Kneeling on soft surface
2. Gently move hips forward and back, side to side, and rotate right and left 30 seconds each
3. Repeat on other side
4. 2-3 times per day

Upper Back Stretch: The upper back most common gets limited in rotation. This gentle stretch is designed to increase rotation in the upper back and relieve stress in the SI Joint.

How to do it:

1. Lay on your side with knees bent at least 90 degrees
2. Move arm up toward ceiling and gently reach back towards floor
3. Hold 45 seconds

Lateral Hip Stretch: The SI joint is effected by any loss of hip motion. It is very common for the lateral part of the hip or IT band to get tight.

How to do it:

1. Place foot closest to wall forward
2. Slide hip laterally towards the wall
3. Hands on wall for support
4. Move hips gently toward wall with hips side to side 60 seconds

CHAPTER 19

A Special Offer for You

To show you how much I appreciate you taking the time to read this book I want to make you a special offer. I also know that you are dedicated to finding a solution and you will do whatever it takes. Your motivated to find a natural way to heal your lower back pain and you want to avoid or stop taking medications and injections. So with all of that being said I believe that I have a solution for you. I believe that nobody should have to live with lower back pain. So this special offer is for you or anyone you know who might need help finding a permanent solution. I want to invite you to our private Lower Back Pain and Sciatica Workshop. This workshop will answer any questions you have and allow you to learn even more about lower back pain and sciatica from the experts. To register for this Workshop, you simply call 231.944. 6541. Now if you have already been to the workshop or feel it would not be of interest to you for whatever reason the second offer is to have a one on one consult over the phone with me. Same way just simply call my office 231.944.6541 and I would be happy to spend some time with you answering any questions you might have. I hope this book has helped you and that you will take action now to find a permanent solution to your lower back pain and sciatica. Thank you for reading.

CHAPTER 20

About the Author

Andrew Gorecki received his doctorate in physical therapy from Central Michigan University in 2009 as well as his Bachelor of Exercise Science from Northern Michigan University in 2006. Recently Andrew Gorecki has completed a Fellowship in Applied Functional Science in 2013 and is the founder of Superior Physical Therapy in Traverse City, MI. He specializes in lower back pain and sciatica treatment as well as the rest of his staff. As a lower back pain and sciatica sufferer for many years in the past Andrew has a unique perspective as he has received every treatment that is available including surgery, which ultimately failed until he got to the root of the problem (his hips didn't move). Andrew is married to his lovely wife Erin and they have two young children, Max and Gibson. Andrew is dedicated to being the best husband, father, physical therapist, and friend that he can be and is here to serve. If you have any interest in reaching out to Andrew he can be reached by emailing andrewg@thesuperiortherapy.com

Made in the USA
Lexington, KY
11 May 2017